Jordan

by

Dennis P. Eichhorn

A *Reading Success* Paperback Book

Turman Publishing Company
Seattle

Author: Dennis P. Eichhorn
Series Editor: Louise Morgan
Copy Editor: Lori Starrs
Photo Credits: front cover—Noren Trotman, back cover—Bill Smith; B&W photographs: AP/Wide World Photos, Laney High School, Seattle Times, Seattle SuperSonics, Bill Smith, Noren Trotman, University of North Carolina, UPI/Bettman Newsphotos
Harris-Jacobson Rating 4
An Unauthorized Biography

Copyright © 1987 Turman Publishing Company
P.O. Box 19680, Seattle, Washington 98109

All rights reserved.
No part of this book may be reproduced by any means without written permission from the publisher.

Catalog No. 208
Library of Congress Catalog Card Number: 88-50793
ISBN 0-89872-208-X
Printed in the United States of America
Reprinted 1995

CONTENTS

Chapter	Page
1 "I'm slim, trim, and cat-quick."	1
2 "Work hard for what you want."	9
3 'The Last Shot'	17
4 "Things will fall into place."	25
5 All eyes are on Michael.	32
6 "I don't care about setting any records."	40
7 Air Jordan	47
8 Michael Jordan or Dr. J, Jr.?	55
9 Can he be stopped?	63
10 Michael speaks out.	71

NOTE: A glossary of unfamiliar terms is provided at the end of each chapter.

Michael shows how it's done in an NBA slam dunk contest.

CHAPTER 1
"I'm slim, trim, and cat-quick."

Look . . . up in the air! It's a bird! It's a plane! It's super Michael!

Yes, it's Michael Jordan, the superstar guard who plays for the Chicago Bulls of the National Basketball Association. Michael Jordan, the player whom many people believe to be the most talented ever. Michael Jordan, who goes for the hoop with his eyes rolling and his tongue hanging out. The man who seems to hang in the air a little longer than anyone else.

But who is Michael Jordan?

To hear Michael answer that question, you'd think he's no one special. "I'm just a team player," he says. "I want to help out in any way I can so that my team can win. Making the crowd and my teammates happy makes me happy. I love the game. I really do. I enjoy it, and I want others to enjoy it. I never think of it as a job."

But there are other people who think that Michael is very special. Larry Bird is one of those people. "There's no doubt in my mind that when

Michael is healthy, he's the best player in the league," says Larry. "What more can I say?"

Coming from Larry, that's high praise. Larry isn't the only player to be amazed at what Michael can do with a basketball. Sidney Green, one of Michael's teammates on the Chicago Bulls, has this to say: "Michael is the truth, the whole truth, and nothing but the truth when it comes to playing basketball."

It's hard to believe that any player can be praised so highly. After all, in pro basketball today, there are dozens of great players. It seems as if every team has at least one superstar. What has Michael done that makes people call him the best?

After a promising start as a high school athlete and student in Wilmington, North Carolina, Michael entered the University of North Carolina. He turned out for the Tar Heels basketball team and came to national attention during the last game of his freshman season. With 17 seconds left, Michael hit a long shot that gave North Carolina a one-point win over Georgetown and the 1982 national college basketball championship. Suddenly, Michael was a star.

"Sometimes, it seems as if I've got the ability just to be in the right place at the right time," says Michael. "That 1982 game is one example."

People were predicting great things for Michael, and he didn't let them down. He was chosen college player of the year by *Sporting News* both his sophomore and junior years, 1983 and 1984.

"I'm slim, trim, and cat-quick."

Michael led the United States basketball team to a first-place finish in the 1983 Pan-American Games. Then he led the United States team to a gold medal in the 1984 Olympics. By that time, Michael was one of the best-known sports stars in the world.

Michael stayed in the public eye by becoming a professional. He was chosen by the Chicago Bulls in the 1984 college draft and went right to work. Michael became the Bulls' team leader. He was voted the NBA's rookie of the year. At the same time, he led the Bulls in blocked shots, rebounds, and assists. Michael was also the year's top scorer in the NBA. No one could deny that Michael had become a star among stars.

With every season, Michael seemed to get better and better. Even though he was slowed down by an injury during his second season, he still led the Bulls in scoring. Michael was used to winning games. But the Bulls needed some work before they could become NBA champs. "I have to be a man and accept losing," he says, "but it's very hard for me."

The more basketball fans saw of Michael, the more they liked him. Everywhere the Bulls went to play, crowds of people followed the team. Fans would knock players down, trying to get near Michael. Sometimes they would tear his clothes off. "Traveling with Michael Jordan is like being

Michael soars over the Brazilians during the 1983 Pan American Games. Michael led the United States team to a first-place finish.

"I'm slim, trim, and cat-quick."

on tour with The Jacksons," says Orlando Woolridge, the Bulls' All-Star power forward. "He's Michael, and we're the Jacksons."

Unlike most other great players, Michael doesn't have a nickname. Once, some of his childhood friends called him 'The Rabbit,' but that didn't last long. The Bulls tried calling him 'Mr. Jordan,' but Michael didn't go for that name. "My father is 'Mr. Jordan,' " he says. Others have tried calling him 'Air Jordan.' But he doesn't like that, either. "That's my shoes, not me," says Michael. "I never had a nickname before, and I don't need one now."

How does Michael see himself? "I'm slim, trim, and cat-quick," he says. "My style is Michael Jordan's. I didn't copy it after anyone else.

"I'm doing the things I normally do and playing my natural game. Once I'm on the court, it's really fun. Believe me, I'm very grateful that a lot of people respect me for my ability, but it's equally important that people respect me as a man."

That's Michael Jordan, one of the finest basketball players ever to play the game . . . and a man who deeply cares what people think. This is his story.

Glossary

This glossary gives an explanation of how certain words were used in this book. A more complete definition of each word can be found in a dictionary.

ability: skill.
accept: be able to live with.
among: with others.
assists: giving the ball to another player on his team who scores.
athlete: someone who plays sports.
attention: notice from others.
championship: award won by the best team.
champs: the best team.
childhood: the time he was a child.
chosen: picked.
clothes: what he wears.
college: school after high school.
crowd: people who go to watch the games.
deny: say it's not true.
doubt: idea that he might be wrong.
dozens: lots.
effort: amount of energy he puts into the game.
either: one of two things.
enjoy: like.
everywhere: all places.
example: something that proves a point.
freshman: first year.
grateful: thankful; glad.
guard: player on a basketball team.

"I'm slim, trim, and cat-quick."

healthy: feeling good.
hoop: basketball basket.
important: something that means a lot.
injury: hurt or damage to his body.
junior: third-year.
leader: most important player.
league: group of professional basketball teams.
least: not less than.
medal: prize.
National Basketball Association: group of professional basketball teams in the U.S.
natural: true, not fake.
nickname: special name.
normally: in a regular way.
player: person on the team.
power forward: a player on a basketball team.
praise: saying he is a good player.
predicting: saying what would happen.
professional: someone who is paid for playing a sport.
promising: showing signs of future success.
public eye: where he would be seen by people.
rebounds: getting the ball after someone has missed a shot.
respect: look up to.
rookie: first-year player.
season: one year's worth of basketball games.
sophomore: second-year.
student: someone who goes to school.
style: his own way of playing.

superstar: one of the best.
talented: able to play well.
teammates: other players on the team.
tongue: part of the mouth.
truth: what is true.
university: school after high school.
whole: all of something.

CHAPTER 2
"Work hard for what you want."

Michael Jeffrey Jordan was born on February 17, 1963, in Brooklyn, New York, and was raised in Wilmington, North Carolina. His mother, Delores Jordan, was a customer service rep for the United Carolina Bank. Michael's father, James Jordan, was a plant supervisor for General Electric. The fourth of five children, Michael has two brothers and two sisters. "I was lucky," says Michael. "I have parents who care. They gave me guidance and taught me to work hard. I've learned my lessons."

The Jordan family wasn't poor, but as in most families, there never seemed to be enough money to go around. The five Jordan kids had to learn to go without some of the things they wanted. "I was 16 when I got my first bicycle," Michael remembers. "I used to get angry that I didn't have one. But we didn't have a lot of money, and I think my parents wanted me to appreciate it when I finally got one. I almost slept with that bicycle when I finally got it."

As a high school freshman, Michael branched out into many sports—baseball, football, and track—eventually concentrating on basketball.

As a young boy, Michael grew to love sports. At first, he played Little League baseball. Right from the start, Michael played to win. "He gets his competitive nature from his mother," says his father. "She's a winner."

At Laney High School, Michael branched out into other sports. Not only did he play shortstop and outfield for the school baseball team, he also pitched some no-hitters. Michael turned out for

"Work hard for what you want."

track and did well at both the long jump and high jump. Michael became the quarterback for the school football team. But after a couple of football injuries, his mother had a talk with him. "Couldn't you try a less dangerous sport?" she asked. That's when Michael decided to give basketball a little more attention.

Michael and his younger brother Larry would play basketball for hours on the court their father built in their backyard. "Larry always used to beat me on the backyard court," says Michael. "His vertical jump is higher than mine. He's got the dunks and some 360s and most all of the same stuff that I've got. At only five-seven, Larry is my inspiration!"

Michael wasn't very tall then, himself. As a sophomore at Laney High School, he stood six feet, one inch tall. He kept working on his basketball skills, and he kept growing. By the time Michael graduated from high school, he was six feet, six inches tall. He had developed many of the moves that were to make him a superstar.

"When you're young, you don't realize that you've got the skill," Michael says. "People ask me where I got it, and I can't tell them. The one thing that I did develop on my own was determination. I got that when I was very small."

Michael could never walk away from basketball," remembers his father. "He'd just play and play and play. In our family we try to make something happen, rather than waiting around for it to happen. We believe the surest way to success is to work hard for what you want."

At first, Michael had a hard time making the high school varsity team. "I was disappointed because a friend of mine made the varsity and I didn't," he says. "I averaged 27 or 28 points a game on the junior varsity team. When the varsity went to the play-offs, I thought I'd be called up. But I wasn't. When the team went to the regionals, the coach let me on the bus only because a manager got sick. I didn't have a ticket to get into the game, so I had to carry the uniform of our star player to get in. I didn't want that to happen again.

"From that day on, I just worked on my basketball skills. Then I grew. I grew so quickly, I couldn't keep up with my skills. But I still averaged 25 points as a junior. My coach finally got tired of this kid hanging around trying to get better. So he started picking me up at 8 a.m. every day, and we'd go to the gym to work on my skills. Then I would take a shower and go to class. We did that every day."

By the time Michael graduated from high school, he was a star. Many college coaches wanted him to attend their schools. It was time for Michael to look around and make a decision.

"Work hard for what you want."

Michael's coach worked with him every morning before school. By the time he graduated, Michael was a star for Laney High School.

Glossary

This glossary gives an explanation of how certain words were used in this book. A more complete definition of each word can be found in a dictionary.

appreciate: understand what something is worth.
attend: go to.
attention: notice from others.
averaged: made about that many.
baseball: sport played with a ball and bat.
beat: win.
bicycle: machine with two wheels that a person rides.
built: made.
coach: teacher of a sport.
competitive: wants to win.
couple: two.
court: place where basketball is played.
customer service rep: job at the company.
dangerous: something that could cause him to get hurt.
decided: made up his mind.
decision: choice.
determination: not giving up.
develop: work to get better.
disappointed: sad about not getting what he wanted.
dunks: way to score points in basketball by stuffing the ball down through the hoop.
finally: after a long wait.

"Work hard for what you want."

football: sport with running, passing, tackling, and hard-hitting body contact.
graduated: finished.
guidance: advice on how to do something.
gym: building where sports are played.
inch: small measure.
injuries: damage to his body.
inspiration: something that makes him try harder.
junior varsity: a school's second-best team.
kid: a young person.
Little League: group of teams for young people.
manager: person who helps run a sports team.
nature: way of doing things; personality.
no-hitters: baseball game in which the pitcher doesn't allow the other team to get any hits.
outfield: defensive position on a baseball team.
pitched: played pitcher on a baseball team.
play-offs: part of the championship games.
player: person on a team.
quarterback: player on a football team.
raised: grew up.
rather: instead of.
realize: know.
regionals: part of the championship games.
shortstop: defensive position on a baseball team.
shower: wash off.
skill: ability to do things well.
sophomore: tenth-grade student.
supervisor: person in charge.

ticket: slip of paper that gets someone into a game.
uniform: what team players wear.
varsity: school's best team.
vertical: in an up-and-down direction.

CHAPTER 3
'The Last Shot'

After looking at dozens of college campuses, Michael decided to go to the University of North Carolina. "I didn't choose to go there because of basketball, either," he says. "I visited the campus as part of Project Uplift, a state program for students. I saw the school as a student, not as an athlete. Sometimes, athletes are shown only the good parts of a school that's trying to get them. But that didn't happen to me. I decided the University of North Carolina fit my lifestyle.

"In fact, when I was growing up, I hated the University of North Carolina. I was a North Carolina State fan; David Thompson was the man. My mom liked Phil Ford, but I couldn't stand him or any of those other Carolina guys. But that was out of my system by the time I was ready to go to college. As I said, the coaches didn't even know that I was looking the campus over. I saw everything as a potential student, not as an athletic recruit."

Michael did know Coach Dean Smith and several of the players. He'd met Buzz Peterson, who became his roommate and Tar Heel team-

While at the University of North Carolina, Michael became famous for 'The Last Shot'—a 16-foot jump shot that clinched UNC's one-point victory in the 1982 national championship game.

mate, at a summer basketball camp given by Coach Smith a few months before Michael started school. "I'll never forget it," says Buzz. "Michael said, 'This is my first camp, and I'm scared.' We laugh about it now."

Buzz continues, "We met again at Five-Star Camp later that summer. It was the best-known summer basketball camp in the area. Michael won five trophies. The camp staff invited him back the following week, and he won four more.

"What impressed me about Michael was his love for his parents and his family. He was a fun guy to be around, too. All that ends when he goes on the court, though. That's when he becomes deadly serious."

Buzz and Michael became very good friends. "It's a beautiful friendship," says Michael's father. "From the moment we met Buzz's parents at the summer camp, we hit it off. We've always considered Michael's friends as our sons, and we advise them as we do Michael."

As a freshman guard on the Tar Heel team, Michael had a good year. He averaged 13.5 points and 4.4 rebounds a game. But Michael still had a lot to learn. His play on defense, for one thing, wasn't as good as he wanted it to be. Yet no one doubted that Michael would be a star at the University of North Carolina in the years ahead.

Then, with 17 seconds left in the 1982 national championship game, Michael made the famous 16-foot jump shot that clinched UNC's one-point victory over Georgetown. The Tar Heels were national champs, and Michael was famous. "Everyone called it 'The Last Shot,'" says Michael. "For a while it was a big deal at the University of North Carolina. The cover of the Chapel Hill telephone book, for instance, had a photo of me making 'The Last Shot' on it.

"At first, I enjoyed the public recognition. Three years before, I never would have dreamed that a kid would ask me for an autograph. But at times, the recognition got to be a worry. I would get embarrassed when I was noticed in restaurants. I knew that many people just saw me as the guy who made 'The Last Shot.' To them, I was just Michael Jordan, the star basketball player. When I met a girl socially and saw that she didn't recognize me, I'd just tell her my name was Michael. Then I could carry on a conversation and see how she was acting toward me as a person."

Michael was getting his first taste of stardom. He handled it well. Michael worked hard at his studies, taking classes in speech and cultural geography. He also worked hard at becoming a better basketball player.

Michael had grown into a fine athlete. He was six feet, six and one-half inches tall, and weighed over 200 pounds. Michael could run 40 yards in 4.38 seconds, faster than most pro football running backs. Basketball lovers everywhere were watching to see just how great Michael was going to become.

'The Last Shot'

Michael was named the top male collegiate basketball player for 1984 and was given the Eastman Award.

Glossary

This glossary gives an explanation of how certain words were used in this book. A more complete definition of each word can be found in a dictionary.

advise: offer ideas about what they should do.
area: nearby places.
autograph: sign his name.
averaged: had about that many.
camp: place where players stay and work on their basketball skills.
campus: school grounds.
clinched: made it final.
considered: thought of.
continues: goes on.
conversation: talking.
court: place where basketball is played.
cultural geography: a college class.
deadly serious: never plays around.
deal: thing.
decided: made up his mind.
defense: play that tries to keep the other team from scoring.
doubted: thought it might not happen.
dozens: lots.
embarrassed: nervous and uneasy.
enjoyed: liked.
famous: well-known.

'The Last Shot'

freshman: first-year.
friendship: being friends.
grown: become.
guard: player on a basketball team.
impressed: was affected deeply.
invited: asked him to come.
lifestyle: how he lives.
national championship: game that decides who is the best in the U.S.
noticed: seen.
photo: picture.
player: person on the team.
potential: possible.
pro: short for professional (person who is paid to play a sport).
public recognition: people noticing him.
rebounds: getting the ball after someone misses a shot.
recognize: know who he was.
recruit: person the school would like to have as a student.
restaurants: places where people go to eat out.
roommate: person who shared his room.
several: many.
socially: when he was going out.
speech: a class in speaking well.
staff: people in charge at the camp.
stardom: being a star.
state program: government plan or project.
studies: classes.

system: thoughts.
taste: experience.
trophies: awards.
victory: a win.
weighed: how heavy he was.
worry: something that made him nervous.

CHAPTER **4**
"Things will fall into place."

During his sophomore season, Michael worked hard on his defense. He won the team's defensive player of the game award 13 times. Even while concentrating on his defensive play, Michael still was able to score 20 points a game. He was named college player of the year by *Sporting News* in 1983 and was an All-American team choice.

Michael's junior year was more of the same. Not only did he earn the title of college player of the year for the second time, but Michael once again was everyone's choice as an All-American. He had become one of the best college defensive players in the country at the same time he continued to score 20 points a game.

Michael also was part of the United States team that won a gold medal in the summer Pan-American games. He and Sam Perkins, his teammate from the University of North Carolina, were the two biggest stars on the Pan-Am team.

The Tar Heels didn't win the national championship Michael's sophomore or junior season. But

Jordan

Before the 1984 Olympic Games, the United States team went up against the NBA All Stars. Chris Engler (center) and Magic Johnson (right) had their hands full trying to contain Michael.

the team did play great basketball. Michael, in particular, was getting into a winning groove. His parents hadn't missed a game since his high school days, and they could see how hard he was trying to win. "You're trying to force things," Michael's father told him. "You've got enough talent that if you just play like Michael Jordan, things will fall into place."

Michael took his father's advice. He knew that his game was getting so good that he could play in the pros. He was thinking about giving up his

"Things will fall into place."

senior year of college to become a pro.

Michael finally made up his mind to put off his last year of college to turn pro. "It's hard to give up part of your life, like your senior year in college."

In the 1984 college draft, Michael was the third player picked. He went to the Chicago Bulls. Michael was happy about that, but before he could turn his attention to pro basketball, there was the important matter of the 1984 Olympics. Michael was one of the players chosen to play on the United States men's basketball team.

There were some well-known college stars on the Olympic team. Besides Michael, the team included Patrick Ewing, Wayman Tisdale, and Lorenzo Charles. But it was Michael that everyone was talking about.

The Olympic team was coached by Bobby Knight, an outspoken college coach. For several weeks before the 1984 Olympics, the Olympic team played a team made up of NBA pros to get ready for the games. After a few of the pre-Olympic games, Magic Johnson, of the NBA team, was asked who the best Olympic team member was.

"Michael Jordan," said Magic. "He's head and shoulders above everyone else. He's so talented, you can't do anything more with him. He has so much ability."

"That's right," said Isiah Thomas, another NBA team member. "Jordan certainly can play basketball."

Michael and the other United States team members proved their skills by beating Spain 96–65 for the Olympic gold medal. America was proud of the men's team for its fine work. America was proud of Michael for leading the United States team.

With the Olympics behind him, Michael could go to work for the Chicago Bulls.

"Things will fall into place."

The United States Olympic basketball team proved its total domination of the sport with a 96–65 victory over Spain. Michael celebrates with the Olympic gold.

Glossary

This glossary gives an explanation of how certain words were used in this book. A more complete definition of each word can be found in a dictionary.

ability: what he is able to do.
advice: what his father told him to do.
award: prize.
beating: winning over.
choice: person picked for the team.
concentrating: focusing on.
continued: kept on.
defense: play that tries to keep the other team from scoring.
draft: time when pro teams hire new players.
during: at the time of.
finally: in the end.
force: try too hard.
head and shoulders above: is much, much better than the others.
important: means a lot to him.
in particular: especially; more than anyone else.
included: had.
junior: third-year.
member: person on the team.
national championships: games that decide who is the best in the U.S.
outspoken: bold; speaks his mind.
player: person on the team.

"Things will fall into place."

pro: short for professional (someone who is paid for playing a sport).
proved: showed.
score: make points.
season: time of year basketball is played.
several: many.
since: after that time.
sophomore: second-year.
talent: natural ability.
teammate: another player on the team.
winning groove: winning a lot of games.

CHAPTER **5**
All eyes are on Michael.

The Chicago Bulls were glad to have Michael on their team. They had won 27 and lost 55 games the previous season. Michael said that he was looking forward to playing with the Bulls and working with Coach Kevin Loughery. "If I can play for Coach Bobby Knight in the Olympics, I can play for anybody," joked Michael. "Of course, the Chicago Bulls aren't going to be the Michael Jordan show. I'll just be part of the team."

During the exhibition season and into the opening games of the 1984–85 season, Michael worked hard to learn the Chicago system. He soon mastered it, and the Bulls began winning games. At first, it seemed strange to Michael to be playing against NBA superstars week after week. "When I go against guys who have gotten a lot of publicity, I always consider myself the lowest on the totem pole," said Michael. "That makes me work harder, because I want to get to the top.

"All of these guys are legends: Dr. J, Larry Bird, Isiah Thomas, Magic Johnson. They all are above

All eyes are on Michael.

As a pro player with the Chicago Bulls, Michael received the NBA's rookie of the year trophy. Michael had led the Bulls to their best season in years.

me on the totem pole, and I'm down at the bottom trying to get to where they are. You know how it is when a bunch of kids are playing and a new kid comes along? The new kid feels kind of awkward. That's how I felt. I wanted to earn their respect."

That soon happened. NBA players and coaches could tell that Michael was going to be a great player. "Honestly, Michael is a better player than we thought he would be," said coach Loughery of the Bulls. "That's because his ball handling wasn't exposed in college or at the Olympics. Nobody knew he was capable of playing the lead guard spot, but he is.

"You don't have to mess with his head, either. He's got his head together. Michael likes to score points. He thinks about scoring."

"Sure I think about scoring, but being a defensive player is very important to me, too," said Michael. "I want to be consistent on defense every night. I want to be able to contain the offensive player every night. That's my number-one goal, right now."

Michael kept working on his game, and the Bulls seemed like a new team. Fans poured into Chicago for the games, and ticket sales zoomed. Michael was mobbed wherever he went. "People have been cheering me ever since the Olympics," he said. "I expected a warm reception in Chicago. But as for those crowds on the road, I can't express how good it feels to hear their cheers."

The tough style of ball in the NBA took some getting used to. "I was a little surprised at how much physical contact there is," says Michael. "I had to learn not to lose my style of game when that was going on. It did get frustrating, but I learned to deal with it.

"I didn't feel any pressure or feel like I had to prove anything. I just went out and played my game and waited to see what would happen."

What happened was the best basketball that Chicago fans had seen in years. Other coaches said

All eyes are on Michael.

they liked it when their teams played Chicago because people would come out just to watch Michael.

Lenny Wilkens, a former NBA All-Star guard, was then coaching the Seattle SuperSonics. He, too, was amazed at Michael's basketball skills. "Some of Michael's moves are so subtle that only someone who has played in the NBA would know what I was talking about," said Coach Wilkins. "It's the way Michael uses his hands and his body to create shots for himself. It's the same kind of clever stuff that Oscar Robertson and Jerry West used when they played pro ball.

"Another thing I like about Michael is that he understands and likes to play defense. That's unusual in rookies. But people will talk mostly about his offense, of course.

"Like David Thompson, Michael is a leaper who will go right over you to score. I'll tell you this: by the time Michael is through, he will be a much better overall player."

Coach Wilkins was right. Michael led the Bulls to their best season in years, and he was chosen rookie of the year.

Glossary

This glossary gives an explanation of how certain words were used in this book. A more complete definition of each word can be found in a dictionary.

against: opposite.
amazed: surprised.
awkward: uneasy; unsure.
bunch: group.
capable: able.
cheers: clapping and shouts of people who like him.
chosen: picked.
coaching: being in charge of a team.
consider: think of.
consistent: good every game.
contain: keep from scoring.
create: make.
crowds: lots of people.
deal: handle.
defense: play that tries to keep the other team from scoring.
exhibition season: time before real season starts.
expected: thought this would happen.
exposed: shown.
express: say.
former: from the past.
frustrating: made him mad.
goal: something he wants to do.
gotten: had.

All eyes are on Michael.

honestly: really; telling the truth.
important: means a lot.
lead guard: player on a basketball team.
leaper: someone who can jump very high.
legends: people everyone has heard about.
looking forward: excited about the future.
mastered: was able to do it well.
mobbed: had people all around him.
nobody: no one.
of course: as is well known.
offense: points scoring.
offensive: having the ball.
overall: in every way.
physical contact: hitting and bumping into each other.
player: person on the team.
poured into: a lot came in.
pressure: feeling that he had to do something; stress.
previous: one before.
publicity: stories and articles in magazines, newspapers, and on TV.
reception: greeting.
respect: belief that he is good.
rookies: first-year players.
since: after that time.
skills: what he can do well.
stuff: things.
style: way of playing.
subtle: hard to notice.
system: game plans.

ticket: slip of paper that gets someone into a game.

totem pole: something that ranks players from good to bad.

tough: hard to handle; rough.

understands: knows how it should be done.

unusual: different.

wherever: all places.

zoomed: went up very quickly.

All eyes are on Michael.

Michael defies gravity as he goes over Jeff Turner of the New Jersey Nets to score two points.

CHAPTER 6
"I don't care about setting any records."

As Michael's second season in the pros began, he seemed to be better than ever. He'd led the Bulls in scoring, with 28.9 points a game. Michael also led the team in assists, steals, and rebounds. "I compete at everything," said Michael as the season began. "As long as I'm able and in good health, I can go out and compete in anything I set my mind to. I think I could play any professional sport I want to. That's because I'm competitive, and I feel God has given me the ability to adapt to different things very quickly.

"Last year, because I was a rookie, people said a lot of junk about me like I can't do this or I can't do that. I just shrugged my shoulders and went my own way. Basketball is a game, and people are treating it like a war. I'm just going to go out and play and let my playing do all the talking."

That's the way Michael started out, but in the third game of the season, against Golden State, fate stepped in. Michael broke a bone in his left foot.

"I don't care about setting any records."

It would take months for his foot to heal. Michael, who hadn't missed a game all through high school, college, and his rookie year, was shattered. "I wanted to cry for days," he says. "I went into hiding for a while. I couldn't stand traveling with the team knowing that I couldn't play.

"I was a little bit scared. I didn't want to talk to anyone. I didn't want the phone to ring. I didn't want to watch TV or listen to music. I just wanted plain darkness. Not being able to play was hard for me to deal with. It was very painful for me."

Michael returned to North Carolina. The injury had happened in late October, but by February, Michael was working out and shooting baskets. In March he returned to the Bulls' lineup. He had missed 64 games. The Bulls' season ended with 30 wins and 52 losses. But with Michael back, the team won six of its last eight games, making the Bulls eligible for the play-offs.

Michael did everything he could to get the Bulls through the play-offs. He scored 49 points in the first game against the Boston Celtics; then he came back to score 63 points in the second game. It was a play-off record, but the Bulls still lost the series against the Celtics in three games. Michael was so good that Larry Bird, the star Boston player, couldn't seem to praise him enough.

"Michael Jordan is the most awesome player in the league," said Larry. "That was one of the greatest shows of all time. It was one of the greatest in the Boston Garden, on national TV, and

During his second season, Michael broke a bone in his left foot. It would take months to heal. "I wanted to cry for days," he says. "Not being able to play was hard for me to deal with."

"I don't care about setting any records."

in the play-offs. Sometimes I think he's God disguised as Michael Jordan."

Michael took the compliments with a smile. "We all played very well," he said. "In the end, it just came down to who got the breaks and who didn't. But I don't care about setting any records. I'd give all the points back if we could have won.

"There was no pressure on me," Michael went on. "It's just that I was trying to catch up for a lost season. You know how people are. When you're out of sight, people tend to forget you. I'm a competitor, and I like to be respected as a player."

People were giving Michael respect. It was hard to believe that he could come back from a serious injury and still do as well as he did. "Last season made me grow up," Michael said after the play-offs. "If I get hurt again, I'll know how to deal with it. I realize that at some point in time, I'll have to put the ball down and do something else.

"But until then, or until someone who's better than me comes along and takes my place, I'm here. While I'm here, I'm going to play the best I can. I'm paid to be a basketball player, and that's what I want to do—play basketball."

That's exactly what Michael has done. As his career has continued, he's helped the Chicago Bulls become a team to be reckoned with in the NBA. Michael has proven that he can play basketball with anyone in the world and come out on top.

Glossary

This glossary gives an explanation of how certain words were used in this book. A more complete definition of each word can be found in a dictionary.

ability: skill.

adapt: change.

against: opposite.

assists: giving the ball to another player who scores.

awesome: very good.

broke: split into two pieces.

compete: play against.

competitive: wants to win.

competitor: person who wants to win.

compliments: good things said about him.

continued: gone on for some time.

cry: weep; show how sad he was.

darkness: without light; blackness.

deal: handle.

disguised: dressed up to look like someone else.

eligible: able to go.

fate: a power that people cannot change.

forget: don't remember.

given: let him have something.

heal: get better.

health: how his body feels.

injury: hurt or damage to his body.

junk: bad things.

league: group of professional basketball teams.

"I don't care about setting any records."

lineup: players on the team.

losses: games he didn't win.

months: a long time.

national: seen all across the U.S.

painful: hurts a lot.

phone: short for telephone.

plain: simple.

play-off: one of the games that decides who is the best team.

player: person on the team.

pressure: a feeling that he had to do something; stress.

professional: sport in which players get paid.

pros: short for professionals (sports players who are paid).

proven: shown others that something is true.

rebounds: getting the ball after someone misses a shot.

reckoned: thought about seriously.

record: the best anyone has ever done.

respect: others thinking he is a good player.

returned: went back to.

rookie: first-year player.

score: make.

scoring: making points.

series: many games in a row against the same team.

serious: bad enough that it could end his career.

shattered: made to feel confused and sad.

shooting: putting the ball up to score points.

shrugged shoulders: made a sign to show that he didn't care.

steals: taking the ball from the other team.
tend: are likely to do something.
traveling: going with.
treating: acting toward something a certain way.
war: military battle.
won: finished the game with more points than the other team.

CHAPTER **7**
Air Jordan

Everyone knows that sports stars make a lot of money. They get good wages for playing, but that isn't the only way sports stars become rich. They also make money through commercials. Companies like to have sports stars sell their products. When a star is very popular, he or she might make more money from ads than from playing.

Michael is one such sports figure: he makes more from allowing his name to be used for ads than he does from playing basketball. The more famous he becomes, the more money his name is worth. In 1984, after leading the United States team all the way to a gold medal in the Olympics, Michael was very well known. His college career had made him famous, too. When Michael signed with the Chicago Bulls, he could begin to make money from commercials. He signed up with ProServ, a company that finds deals for athletes such as Michael. Michael also started his own company to look after his business interests. He

Jordan

Because Michael seems to fly when he makes a dunk, he was a big success advertising Nike shoes.

Air Jordan

called it J.U.M.P. (Jordan Universal Marketing and Promotions).

ProServ has had many famous athletes for clients—tennis stars, golfers, baseball players, and now, Michael. David Falk, a lawyer who is one of the top people at ProServ, was glad to have Michael for a client. David went to work thinking up ways to make money for Michael.

One day, just before Michael went off to his first Bulls training camp, David met with Rob Strasser, a vice president of Nike. Nike is a big company that makes shoes, clothing, and other athletic equipment. David and Rob discussed their ideas for Nike and Michael Jordan.

Rob told David about a new shoe that Nike was about to put on the market. It would have an air-sole and would be useful to players who do a lot of jumping and running. David liked the plan for the new Nike shoe. He thought it would look good on Michael Jordan.

"Air Jordan," David said. Those words were going to be heard often in the years to come. Michael gave his name to Nike to use on the new line of shoes, and he began to wear them himself. Ads for Air Jordan appeared everywhere.

The first time Michael wore the Air Jordan shoes in an NBA game, he got into trouble with the league. As soon as Michael walked out onto the floor, the referee called a technical foul on him. For the first time in his life, Michael was called for clashing.

You see, the NBA is a very style-conscious league. It has rules about the colors NBA players can and cannot wear together. The Bulls have white uniforms with red and black trim to wear at home and red uniforms with white and black trim to wear on the road. They wear white shoes with red trim. Michael's black Air Jordan shoes with red slashes on the sides broke NBA rules. Wearing those shoes could have cost Michael $1,000 the first time and another $5,000 the next time he did it. But Nike made him some new shoes that were the right colors, and everything came out all right.

Meanwhile, Air Jordan shoes were becoming a very hot item. Nearly half a million pairs were sold in the first month. "They're like Cabbage Patch Dolls," said one excited shoe store owner. "People are buying them even if they're the wrong size, just to have them."

Michael was paid a lot of money by Nike, as much as $2.5 million dollars over five years. Other companies also were paying him money to sell their products. Wilson, a sporting goods company, paid him $200,000 for using his signature on basketballs the company sold. Michael's name also is used by McDonalds, Chevrolet, and Coca-Cola. His name and picture are everywhere: on TV, in newspapers and magazines, and on billboards. Sometimes, it gets a little unreal, even for Michael.

"It is strange," he says. "When I see myself blown up giant-size on a billboard or see myself on TV in an ad, it's a little bit like seeing another person. It's like I'm seeing another part of me I didn't know about before."

Michael keeps busy. When he isn't playing basketball, he probably is off somewhere making a commercial. He has made quite a few, but there is one that strikes Michael as unusual.

"That was the one for Girl Scout Cookies," Michael recalls with a smile. "Tell me that wasn't crazy! It was a radio spot, and I had to read it. It felt really funny because I never sold them before, you know. For some reason, I was never in the Girl Scouts."

From Girl Scout Cookies to Air Jordan shoes, Michael's name is worth money to the companies that pay him to advertise their products. Of course, it's all because of what he can do on the basketball court.

Jordan

Michael finds the going rough as Pacers Steve Stipanovich (left) and Kenton Edelin (right) defend the basket.

Glossary

This glossary gives an explanation of how certain words were used in this book. A more complete definition of each word can be found in a dictionary.

allowing: letting.

appeared: could be seen.

athletes: sports players.

athletic equipment: things used by people to play sports.

billboard: ad on a sign on the side of the road.

blown up: made bigger.

business interests: ways of making money.

camp: place where players stay and work on their skills.

career: time in college.

clashing: wearing something that is not part of the team's game clothes.

clients: people who pay a company to do something.

commercial: ad.

company: a business.

cost: how much he would have to pay.

crazy: silly.

deals: ways to make money.

discussed: talked about.

everywhere: all places.

famous: well-known.

giant-size: huge.

golfers: people who play golf.

half a million: 500,000 or so.

item: thing.

Jordan

lawyer: person who knows all about the law.
league: group of professional basketball teams.
magazines: paper cover book that comes out every so often.
market: where people can buy things.
meanwhile: at the same time.
month: about 30 days.
newspapers: written news that comes out on large sheets of paper every so often.
often: many times.
popular: well known and liked.
radio spot: time on the radio.
reason: why he didn't join.
referee: person who makes sure players don't break the rules.
rich: have a lot of money.
signature: his name as he signs it.
size: how big they are.
slashes: stripes.
somewhere: a place not known now.
style-conscious: thinking a lot about how things look.
technical foul: breaking a rule but not something done while playing.
tennis: game played with racket and ball.
uniforms: what players wear.
unreal: not real.
useful: good for.
vice president: second most important person in the company.
wages: money they make.
worth: how much people will pay for something.

CHAPTER **8**
Michael Jordan or Dr. J, Jr.?

Ever since his days as a player at the University of North Carolina, Michael has been compared to other great players. He's been compared to Oscar Robertson. He's been compared to Jerry West. But more than any other NBA star, Michael has been compared to Dr. J, Julius Erving, of the Philadelphia 76ers.

That's easy to understand. There are two things that Michael and Dr. J have in common: both can dunk the ball from just about any position they choose and both seem to hang in the air a little longer than most other players.

At times, the comparison has bothered Michael. "It's not fair to Michael Jordan or to Julius Erving," he's said. "I'm not trying to follow in his footsteps. Our games are different. I'm trying to create my own identity on the court. But as far as representing a very positive image, I don't mind following Dr. J."

How does Dr. J feel about being compared with Michael? "For me, it is in some ways like looking into a mirror," says Dr. J. "In terms of how creative he is, I see a little of myself in Michael. He takes the ball and attacks. He looks for daylight, and he makes things happen.

"Michael has a lot of charisma. He can fly. He can handle the ball. He makes the steals, he takes the gambles. He does the things that make the crowds expect more. He puts up the stats to back up his showmanship.

"Sure, there will be nights when he has problems. But Michael is a great player. I don't mind being compared to him at all."

How does Michael feel about the things that people are saying? "I'm totally different from Dr. J," he says. "I know his style of defense is totally different. I like to gamble, to help out, and I think that I can play a good one-on-one style, too. I'm not saying Dr. J can't do that, but I'm just speaking for myself.

"I think both of us can shoot. He likes to go out and do fancy dunks and, in turn, I can do the same thing. But I am more of a finesse player, a more fluid type of player. He's taller than I am. He's much stronger and has bigger hands and longer arms. Dr. J will muscle up a player, where I will hang in the air and make some type of move in the air to get a foul. I think I'm going to get fouled a lot more in my pro career than Dr. J. Don't forget that he's a forward, while I'm a shooting guard most of the time. I'll get to handle the ball more, and Dr. J will be under the basket more.

Michael Jordan or Dr. J, Jr.?

According to Dr. J, "Michael takes the ball and attacks. He looks for daylight, and he makes things happen."

Jordan

"There will never be another Dr. J. That's the way it is, and I wouldn't want it any other way. I just want to be my own player. I want to make a name for myself. I don't want to be Dr. J, Jr.

"I have to draw a line between what people expect of me and what I expect of myself. I'm trying to play my natural game. I think I'm making a name for myself with my own style of play and I'm gaining the respect of the other players in the NBA.

"I've always felt that timing plays the most important part in someone's life. If I had come out of school with Dr. J, would I have gotten the same publicity? Probably not. I believe the Good Lord has timing for everyone's life. Luckily, my timing was right: I made a championship-winning shot my first year at the University of North Carolina. I was picked third in the college draft, and I was a star on the Olympic team. With the Bulls, I've gotten a lot of publicity, and I think my skills are up to par. The timing has been right."

The last word on the subject comes from Dr. J himself. The first time he and Michael met, Dr. J had this to say: "Just be yourself and don't worry about comparisons." That's exactly what Michael has done.

Michael Jordan or Dr. J, Jr.?

Often called a one-man wonder, Michael says he is a more fluid type of player than Dr. J.

Glossary

This glossary gives an explanation of how certain words were used in this book. A more complete definition of each word can be found in a dictionary.

attacks: tries very hard to score points.

bothered: made him mad.

career: time he has spent playing basketball.

championship-winning: thing that made his team the best.

charisma: personal charm.

college draft: way pro teams hire players just out of college.

comparison: finding things that are the same and/or different about them.

create: make.

creative: able to do new things.

crowds: people who come to watch games.

daylight: space where no other players are.

defense: play that tries to keep the other team from scoring.

draw a line: separate one thing from another.

dunk: way to score points in basketball by stuffing the ball down through the hoop.

exactly: same thing as.

expect: think will happen.

fancy: hard to do.

finesse: done with skill and grace.

fluid: smooth; moves like water.

footsteps: what Dr. J has done.

Michael Jordan or Dr. J, Jr.?

forward: certain player on the team.
foul: breaking the rules.
gaining: getting.
gambles: risks.
gotten: had.
identity: his own way of playing.
image: how someone is seen by others.
important: means a lot.
in common: both the same.
mirror: something that he looks into and sees himself.
muscle up: play with a lot of pushing and body contact.
natural: true; not fake.
player: person on the team.
position: where the player is.
positive: good.
probably: way something is likely to happen.
problems: things that go wrong.
publicity: stories and articles in newspapers, magazines, and on TV.
representing: standing for; being seen as.
respect: other people thinking he's a good player.
shoot: score points.
shooting guard: player on a basketball team.
showmanship: show of skill.
since: after that time.
speaking: talking.
stats: numbers that measure how well someone plays.
steals: taking the ball from the other team.

style: way he plays.
subject: thing talked about.
totally: very.
type: kind.
understand: know why.
up to par: equal to.
worry: be nervous about.

CHAPTER 9
Can he be stopped?

How would Michael play against a player like himself? "Let's see," he says. "That all depends. If I had a head full of steam, I'd get out of my way.

"But really, it's the same with me as with any strong offensive player. The outside shot is definitely the weaker aspect. If you can get me to miss the first couple of shots from the outside, maybe it will affect me mentally. Of course, if I hit my first two in a row and get my confidence going, that could be the night I score 50 points or more."

It's hard to think of anyone who has ever held Michael in check. But there is one person who can say he did it at least for one game. Is it Larry Bird? Magic Johnson? Dr. J?

No, it's Dan Dakich. Who is he? Well, Dan Dakich played for Indiana, the team that stopped the University of North Carolina in the 1984 NCAA Eastern Regionals. Michael was North Carolina's biggest star at the time. But in that game he only scored 13 points. Dan Dakich was the man who held Michael to that total.

Jordan

Michael hangs for a slam.

Can he be stopped?

"I remember it like it was yesterday," says Dan. "Actually, Michael only scored nine points off me. Then he had a couple of quick scores after I fouled out. But what really happened was I played about five feet off him, and he just missed his first few outside shots. Then he had to sit with foul trouble for a good part of the first half. I did a good job, but it was strictly within the team concept of what we were trying to do.

"I'm a tremendous fan of his now," says Dan. "I watch the news every night instead of *M*A*S*H*, just to see his highlights. When Michael got 63 points against the Celtics, I can remember sitting in my apartment and screaming by myself. I hope he keeps it up and becomes the greatest scorer of all time. Maybe people will remember that I stopped him, for once in his career," says Dan with a laugh.

Some of the stars around the NBA should take lessons from Dan Dakich. He may know something they don't know. So far, no one has figured out a way to keep Michael from scoring. There are some players he has a hard time against, though.

Michael Cooper, of the Los Angeles Lakers, is one of them. "I can't really post him up," says Michael Jordan. "The only other guy I'd say that about is Dale Ellis of the Seattle SuperSonics. When I'm on the move, trying to advance the ball with the dribble, Cooper is very tough. But once I square up to him, I can get by him with the first step.

"Dennis Johnson of the Boston Celtics has very quick hands. But I have quicker feet. I have to protect the ball on the drive, and if I try and cross over in front of him, he'll slap it away. So I try to keep my back to him," Michael continues.

"One guy who has done a good job against me is Detroit's Joe Dumars. He doesn't do anything that differently. Joe makes me drive, and when I do, he stays with me real well. He's hard to post up, but when he relaxes a little, that gives me my edge."

Yes, Michael is very hard to stop. Some would say it's impossible to really stop him. You just have to do your best and stay in his way as much as possible—without drawing any fouls.

Can he be stopped?

Michael is hard to stop. Most players just do their best to stay in his way as much as possible—without drawing any fouls.

Glossary

This glossary gives an explanation of how certain words were used in this book. A more complete definition of each word can be found in a dictionary.

advance: move up the court.
affect: change how he feels.
against: opposite.
aspect: part.
career: time he has been playing basketball.
concept: idea.
confidence: feeling that he can do well.
couple: few.
depends: has to do with many things.
drawing a foul: getting someone to foul.
dribble: bouncing the ball.
Eastern Regionals: eastern part of the national college basketball championship.
edge: advantage.
fan: person who likes Michael.
figured: thought of.
foul: breaking the rules.
guy: man.
highlights: high points; best moments.
impossible: cannot be done.
least: not less than.
lessons: time spent learning.
mentally: in his mind.
of course: as is well known.
offensive: having the ball.

Can he be stopped?

player: person on the team.
possible: can be done.
post up: able to play close to the basket with the ball.
protect: keep something safe.
relaxes: stops paying attention.
scored: made.
scores: points.
scoring: making points.
screaming: cheering and shouting.
slap: hit with his hand.
square: standing face to face.
steam: energy.
strictly: only.
total: final number.
tough: hard to play against.
tremendous: big.
weaker: not as strong.
within: inside of.
yesterday: day before today.

Michael says, "I expected a warm reception in Chicago. But as for those crowds on the road, I can't express how good it feels to hear their cheers."

CHAPTER 10
Michael speaks out.

Sometimes it can be hard to be Michael Jordan. People expect him to be the greatest basketball player in the world, night after night. "I don't try to be a superhuman person," says Michael. "On the court, I try to be the best possible player I can be, of course. Ever since college, people have liked my style of game. I think my personality speaks for itself. I don't think that I go out and do anything to hurt my standing as a role model. I hope people look at me as a player who tries hard and tries to do the best he can at all times. I hope they see that I try to be a good role model for the kids.

"I'm not phony. When reporters ask me questions, I don't take ten minutes to answer, and then sidestep the question. I just say what I feel. If that's the right thing, then I'm just being me.

"I'm very conscious of not letting all the fame and publicity go to my head, too. I've been aware of that ever since I became a pro. I don't want any special treatment, and I never have. I wouldn't want that from other players and I don't want it for myself.

Jordan

"All along, I've said that I don't want the Bulls to be known as Michael Jordan & Company. I'm not trying to overshadow anyone. We're all in this together.

"So far, I've tried to do the same things I did in college and in the Olympics. I don't tell myself that I have to score a certain number of points every night or play a certain number of minutes. Mostly what I've done is try to blend in with the people who already were in the pros.

"I've found that if I just play my natural game, I don't have any trouble pleasing the crowd. Being in the pros has been the most relaxed time of my career. The games come so quickly that if you have a bad one, you can put it behind you and get ready for the next one. When we don't have back-to-back games, I'll replay in my mind what happened the night before. Otherwise, I don't even think about it."

There have been many times that Michael has won a game for his team in the last few seconds. Sometimes, he'll make a play that turns a game around. It looks as if there are times when he surprises even himself.

"That's true," says Michael. "Sometimes I do. When I go up for a shot, I usually don't have any plans other than to find the hoop. Maybe it's better that I don't think too much," he says with a laugh.

"I don't have the attitude of going to look for a situation to take over a game. It's a coincidence

Michael speaks out.

when it happens. Maybe there's just a knack to always being in the right place at the right time. But I don't go out hunting for it. I like it to come to me."

Now that he's a superstar, Michael seems bigger than life to many of his fans. But that isn't what he wants. Michael tries hard to be a person who is no different from anyone else. "When I'm making an appearance in a low-income neighborhood, I talk to guys like they talk to each other. I find myself using the same slang they use. I try to tell them, 'hey, that's part of me, too.' I don't want to seem set apart from them."

What does Michael want from his career? "When it's all over, I hope I can say that I did my best," he says. "I hope that I will have achieved a lot and won a couple of world championships. I think that I'm a winner. My ultimate goal is to help bring a championship to Chicago. I know people laugh and say it will never happen, but it would be a bit foolish to bet against it."

New superstars of the NBA, Michael drives past Dominique Wilkins for a layin.

Michael speaks out.

Glossary

This glossary gives an explanation of how certain words were used in this book. A more complete definition of each word can be found in a dictionary.

achieved: done.
apart: different; not a part of.
appearance: showing up somewhere.
attitude: what he thinks about something.
aware: has thought about.
back-to-back: one right after the other.
bet against: say it won't happen.
blend: mix.
career: time he has spent playing basketball.
certain: fixed.
championships: awards for being the best.
coincidence: something not expected.
conscious: think about a lot.
couple: few.
court: place where the game is played.
crowd: people who come to watch the games.
expect: what they think will happen.
fame: being well known.
fans: people who like Michael.
foolish: dumb.
hoop: basketball basket.
knack: skill.
low-income: without much money.
natural: true, not fake.

Jordan

neighborhood: area where people live.
of course: as is well known.
otherwise: if this is not the case.
overshadow: act like he's more important than the other players.
personality: how he acts.
phony: fake.
player: person on the team.
possible: what can be done.
publicity: stories and articles in newspapers, magazines, and on TV.
relaxed: easy; comfortable.
replay: play again.
reporters: people who report the news.
role model: person others would like to follow.
score: make.
sidestep: avoid; not be honest.
since: after that time.
situation: something happening on the court.
slang: common way of speaking.
special: different from others.
style: way he plays.
superhuman: better than is possible.
superstar: great player.
treatment: how people act toward him.
ultimate: final.
usually: most of the time.